VOL. 2

Eagles

Project Manager: Colgan Bryan
Designer: C. Pacetti
Photography courtesy of: Picture Perfect USA, Inc.

CONTENTS

*As recorded on "Hell Freezes Over."

BITTER CREEK

Words and Music by
BERNIE LEADON

4

6

Verses 2 & 3:

2. Out where the des - ert meets the sky____

3. *See additional lyrics*

is where I___ go___ when I want to hide.___

Oh___ pey - o - te,

(Bkgd:) Oh pey - o - te.

*1st time only

With Fill 2 on Verse 2

To Coda

Fill 2

Guitar 3

8

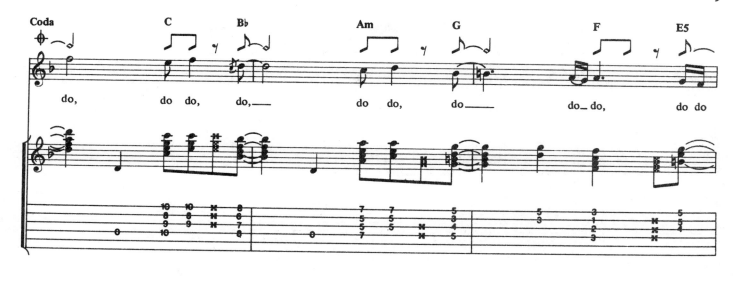

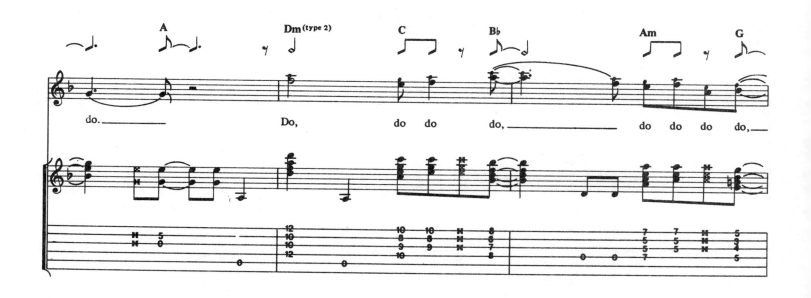

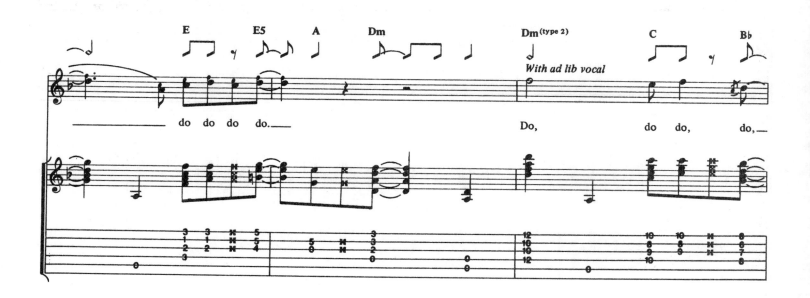

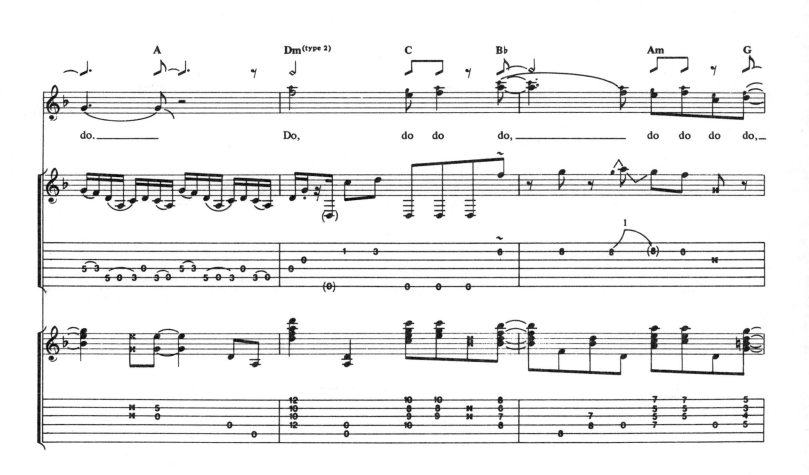

do do do do.___   Do,   do do,   do,___

do do,   do___   do_ do,   do do do.___

Additional lyrics

3. We're gonna hit the road one last time.
   We can walk right in and steal 'em blind.
   All that money (all that money, ooh),
   No more runnin' (no more runnin').

   I can't wait to see the old man's face,
   When I win the race.

DOOLIN - DALTON / DESPERADO
(Reprise)

DOOLIN - DALTON (Reprise)
Words and Music by
**GLENN FREY, JOHN DAVID SOUTHER,
DON HENLEY and JACKSON BROWNE**

DESPERADO (Reprise)
Words and Music by
**DON HENLEY
and GLENN FREY**

*Guitars 1 and 2 arranged for one guitar.

stone cold fact.

Four men ride out and on-ly three ride back.

Interlude: D(type 2)   A(type 2)   Bm   F#m7

*Guitar 4   Guitar 2

With slide

*Banjo arranged for Guitar 4.

D(type 2)   A(type 2)   Bm   rit.

A tempo
F#m(type 2)   F#m7

Guitar 4

Verse: Desperado
F#m7   C#m

(tacet)

The queen of dia - monds let you down she was

Guitar 1

Let ring throughout (finger-style)

Guitar 2

Let ring throughout (finger-style)

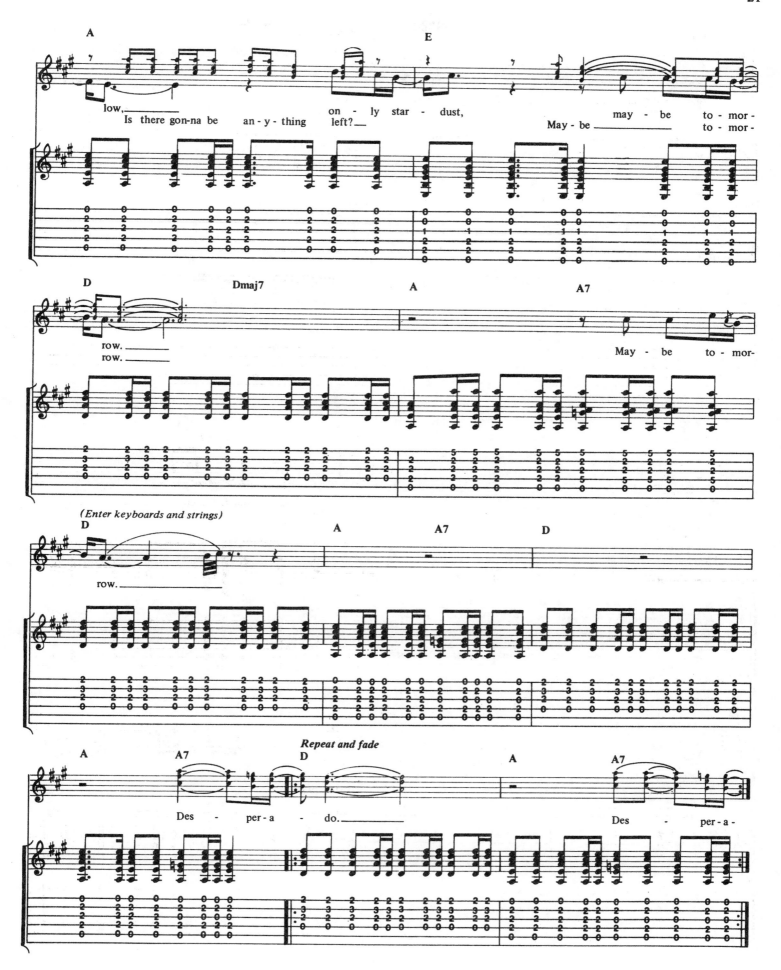

EARLYBIRD

Words and Music by
RANDY MEISNER and BERNIE LEADON

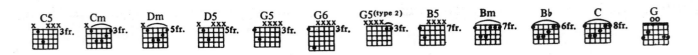

*Banjo arranged for Guitar 1
**Strike strings behind nut.

Intro:

Let ring throughout

G5   G6   G5   G6   G5

Verse 1:
G5   G6   G5   G6   G5

Ear - ly   in   the   morn - in',____   a - bout____   the   break_ of   day,____   the

*Guitar 2
Rhythm Figure 1   End Rhythm Figure 1

*Guitar 1 continues with ad lib variations.

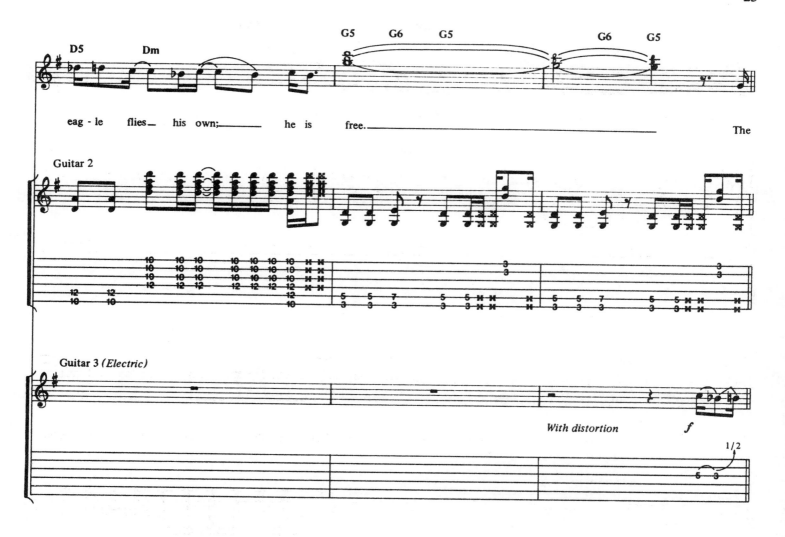

eag - le flies_ his own;____ he is free._____ The

Verse 2:
With Rhythm Figure 1, 4 times

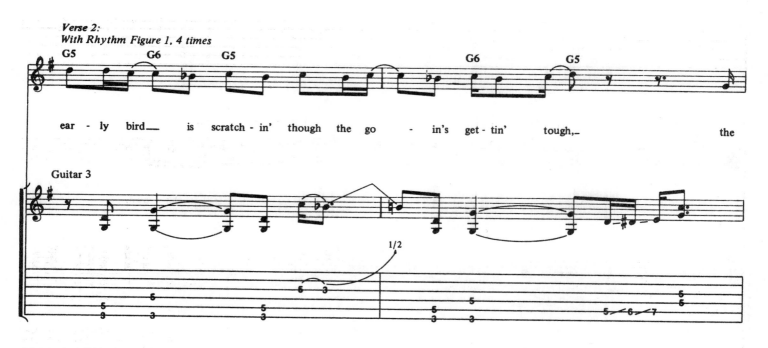

ear - ly bird_ is scratch - in' though the go - in's get - tin' tough,_ the

32

34

36

I WISH YOU PEACE

Words and Music by
PATTI DAVIS and BERNIE LEADON

IS IT TRUE?

Words and Music by
RANDY MEISNER

*Guitar 1 (Center), Guitar 2 (Right), Guitar 3 (Left), Guitar 4 (Center).

When we were young we did-n't real-ly have a care;___ you were hung up,___ I had a good___

50

52

leav - in'._____ Is it true?_____

Is it true?_____

Tacet

LYIN' EYES

Words and Music by
DON HENLEY & GLENN FREY

* Guitar 2 doubled with 6 - string guitar capoed at 5th fret.

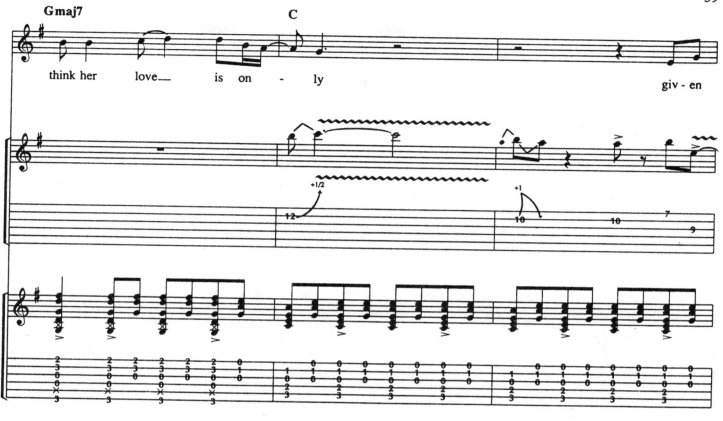

think her love___ is on - ly   giv - en

to a man___ with hands___ as cold___ as ice.___

So she tells him— she must go out— for the eve-

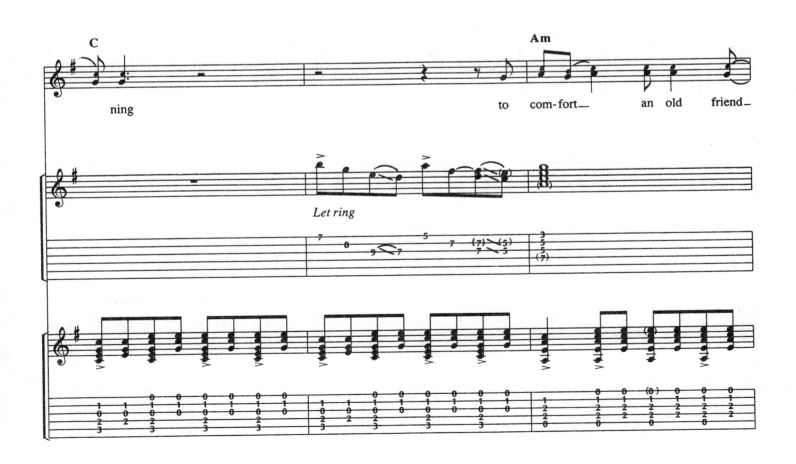

ning

to com-fort— an old friend—

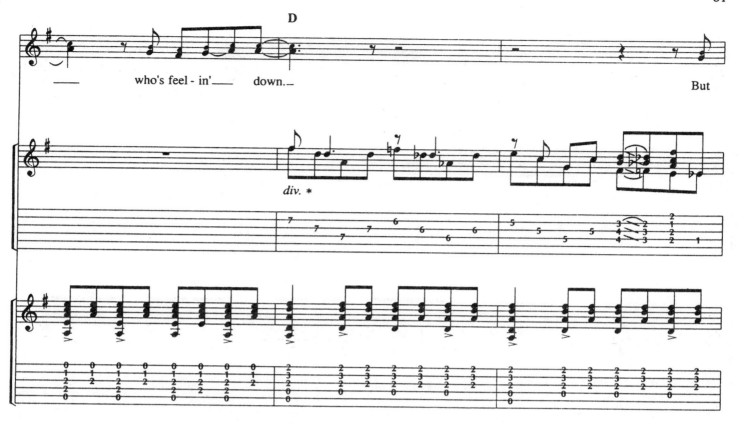

who's feel-in' down.___ But

he knows where___ she's go - in' as she's leav - in';

Lower stemmed notes played by Acoustic.

she is head-ed for___ the cheat-in' side___ of town..

Let ring

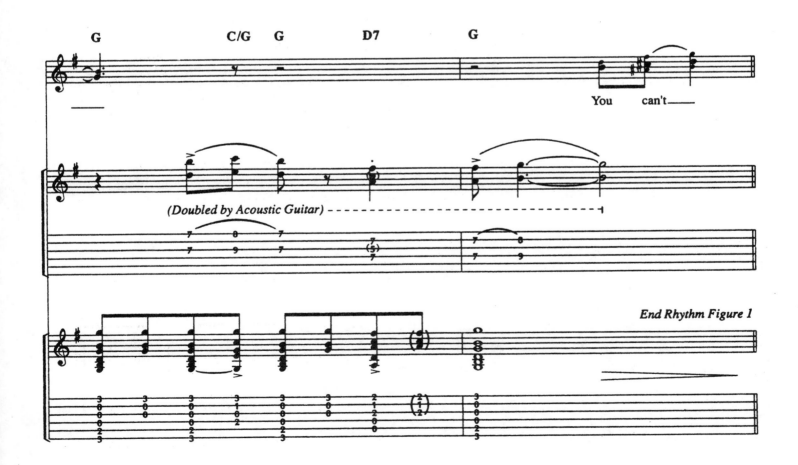

(Doubled by Acoustic Guitar) - - - - - - - - - - - - - - - -

You can't___

End Rhythm Figure 1

Chorus:

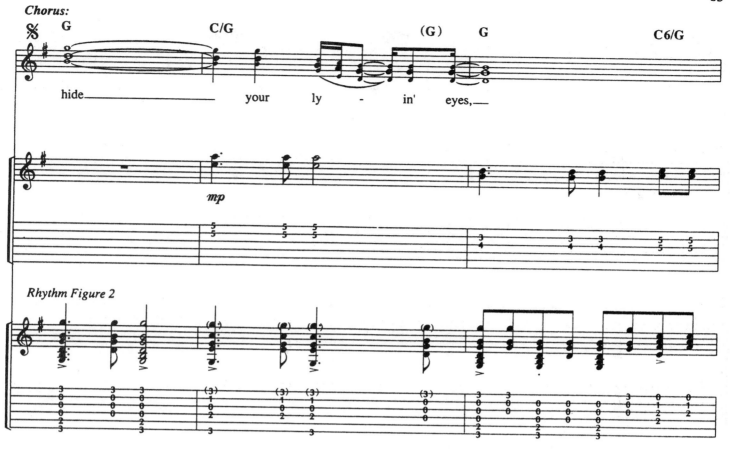

hide_____ your ly - in' eyes,____

Rhythm Figure 2

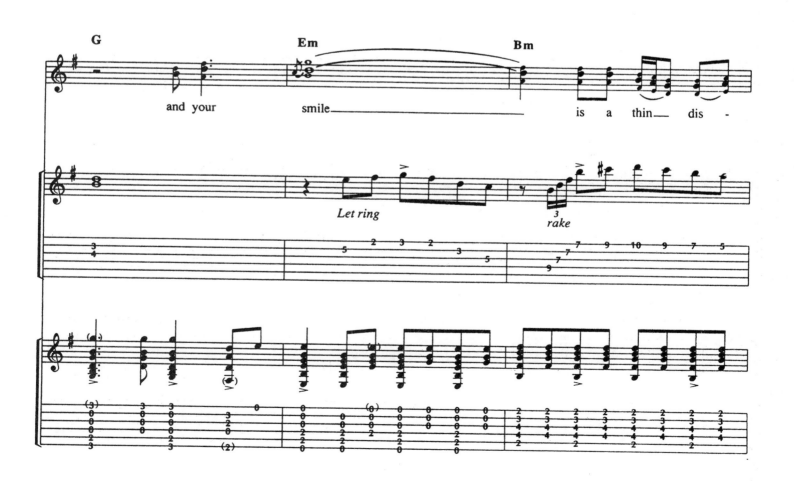

and your smile_____ is a thin__ dis -

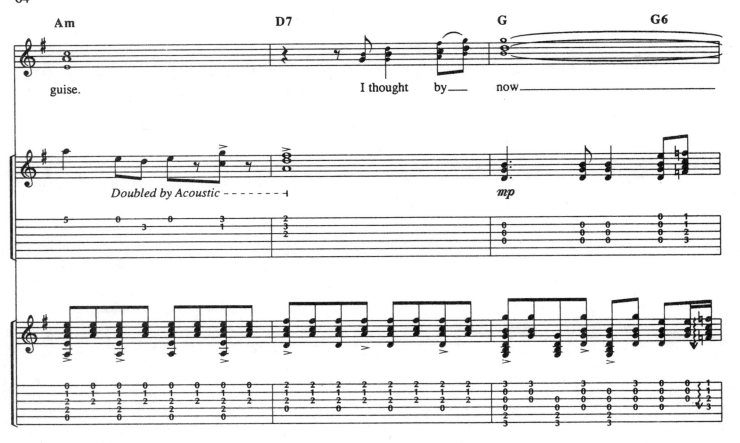

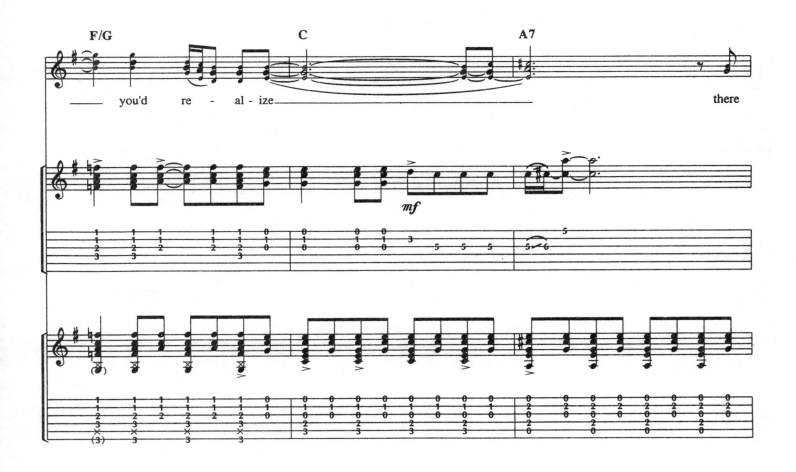

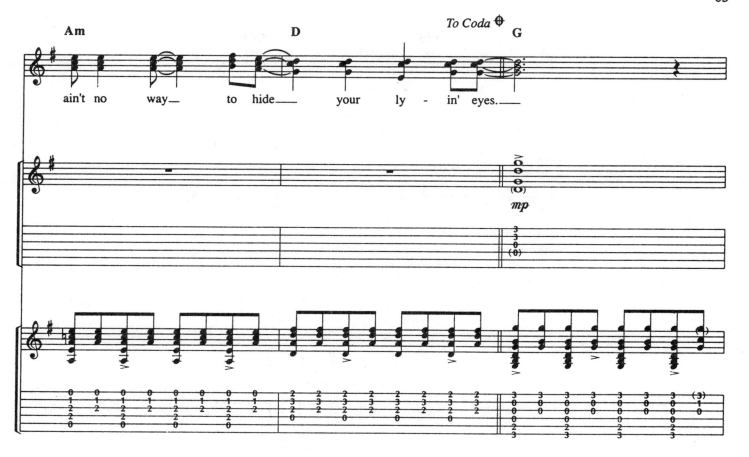

ain't no way__ to hide__ your ly - in' eyes.__

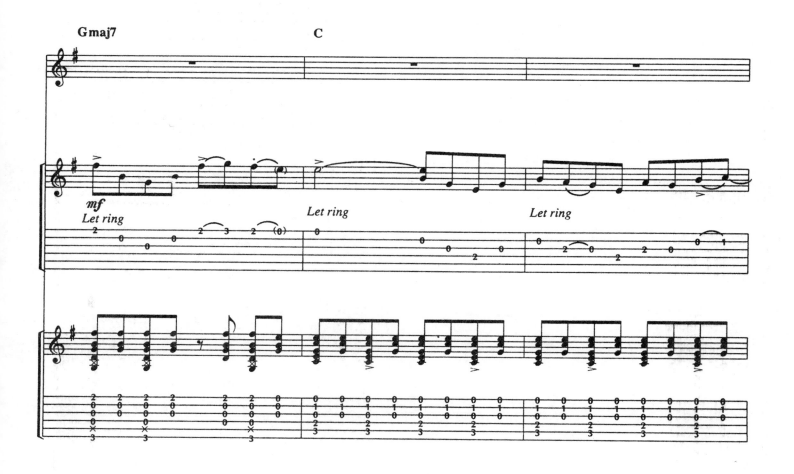

* Up stemmed notes

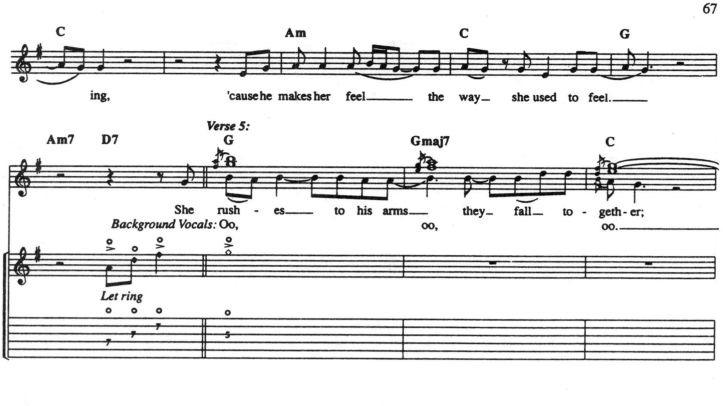

ing,   'cause he makes her feel_____ the way_ she used to feel._____

Verse 5:

She rush - es_____ to his arms_____ they_ fall_ to - geth - er;

Background Vocals: Oo,   oo,   oo._____

Let ring

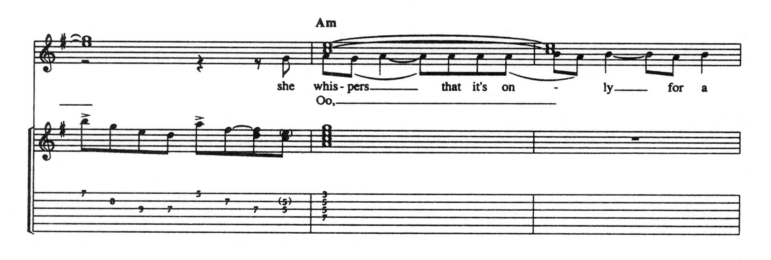

she whis - pers_____ that it's on - ly_____ for a

Oo,_____

while._   She swears that soon_ she'll be

oo._____   Oo,

Let ring

Verse 6:

She gets up___ an' pours___ her-self___ a strong___ one,

an' stares out at the stars_____ up in the___ sky.___

___ An - oth - er night___ it's

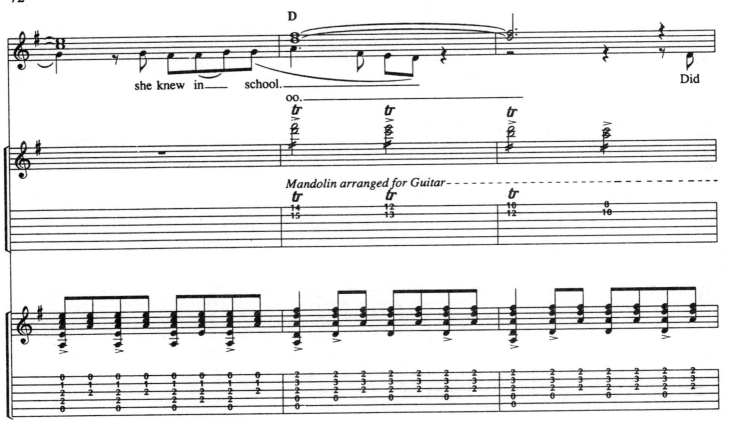

she's so far gone— she feels— just like a fool.—
Oo,——————————————

(Mandolin)

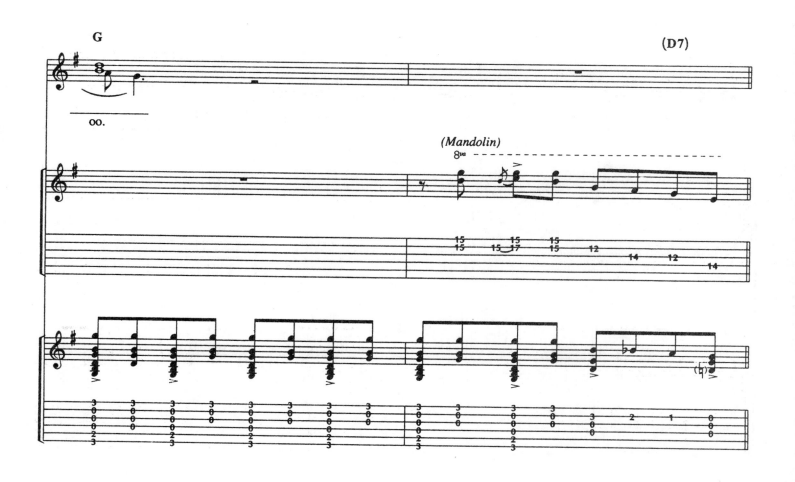

oo.

(Mandolin)

Verse 8:

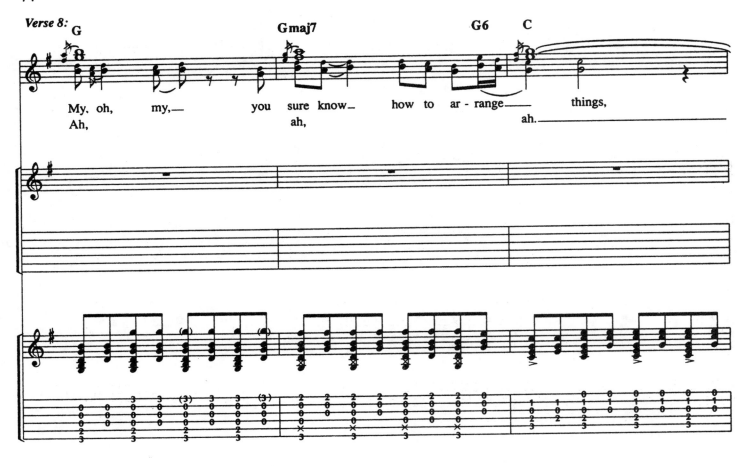

My, oh, my,— you sure know— how to ar - range— things,
Ah, ah, ah.

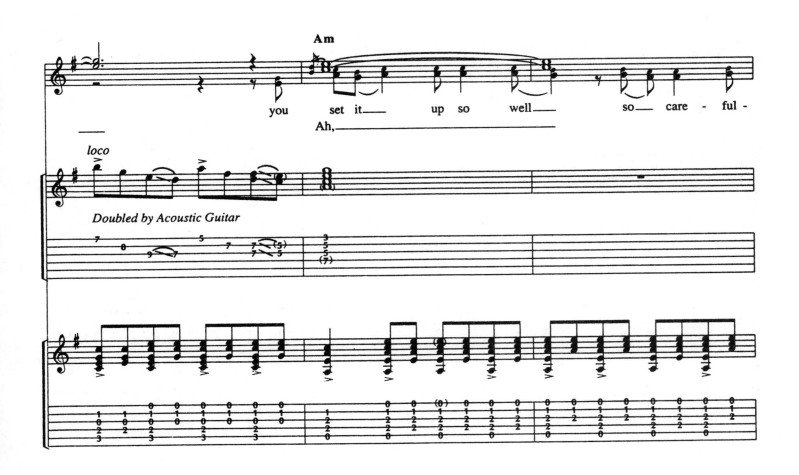

you set it— up so well— so— care - ful -
Ah,

loco

Doubled by Acoustic Guitar

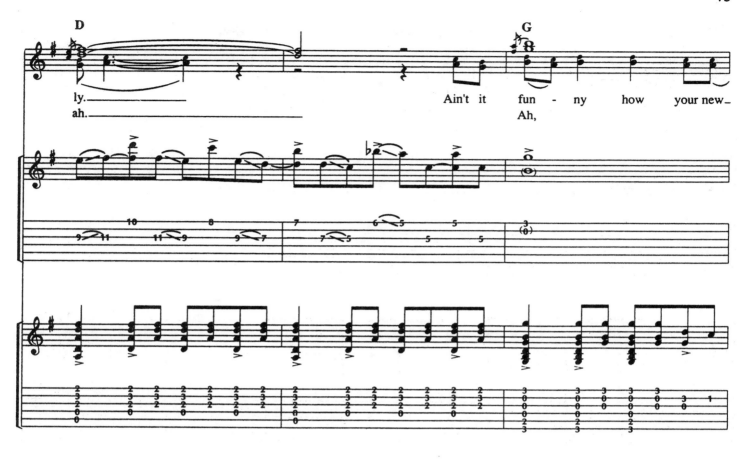

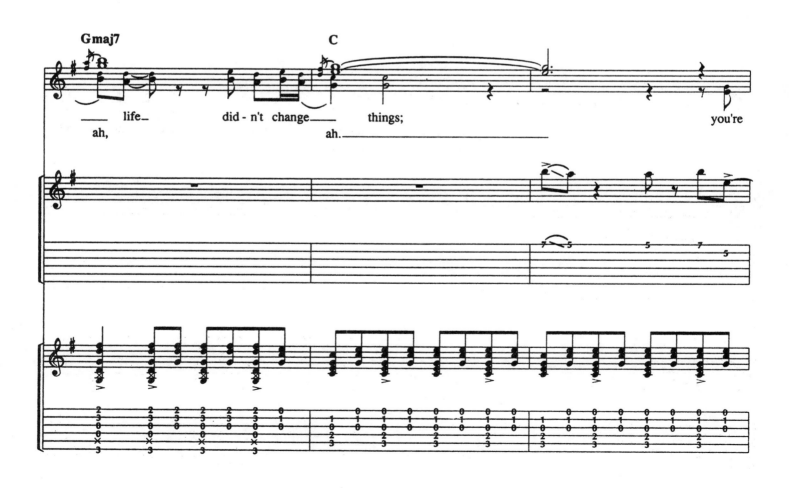

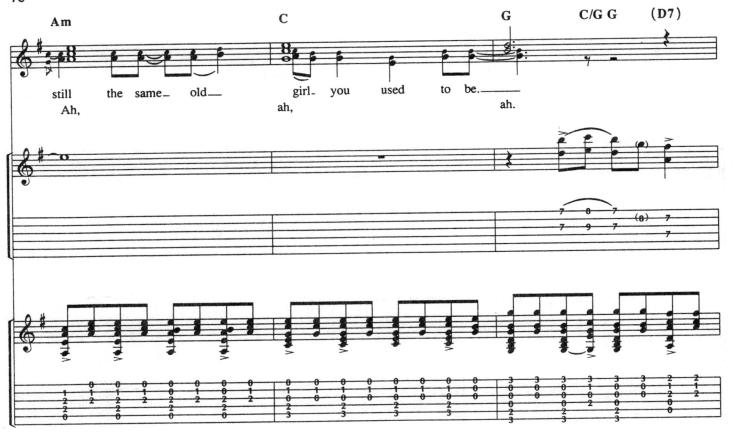

still the same— old— girl— you used to be._____
Ah, ah, ah.

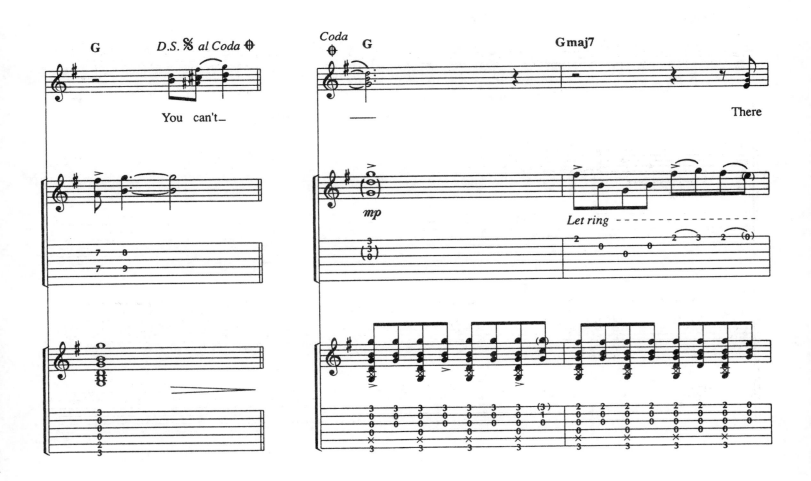

You can't—

There

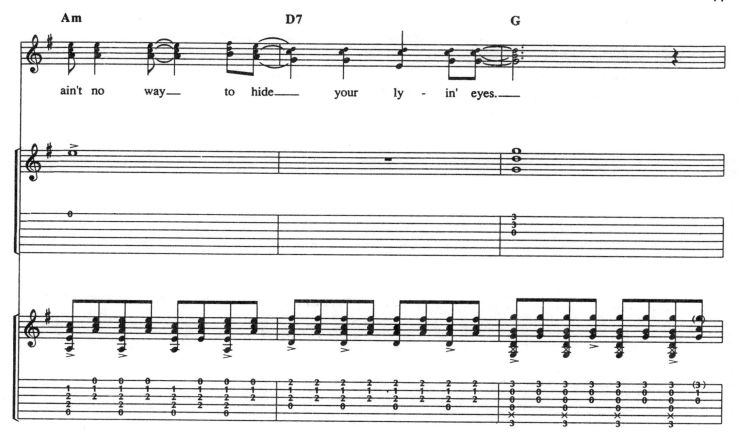

ain't no way—— to hide—— your ly - in' eyes.——

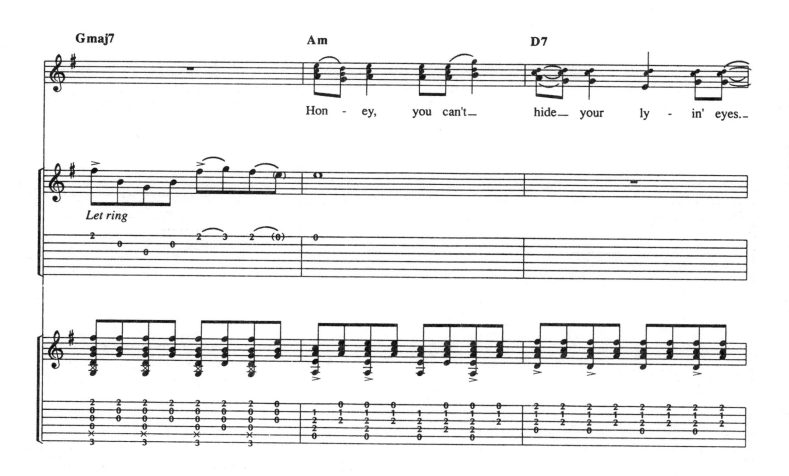

Hon - ey, you can't—— hide—— your ly - in' eyes.——

Let ring

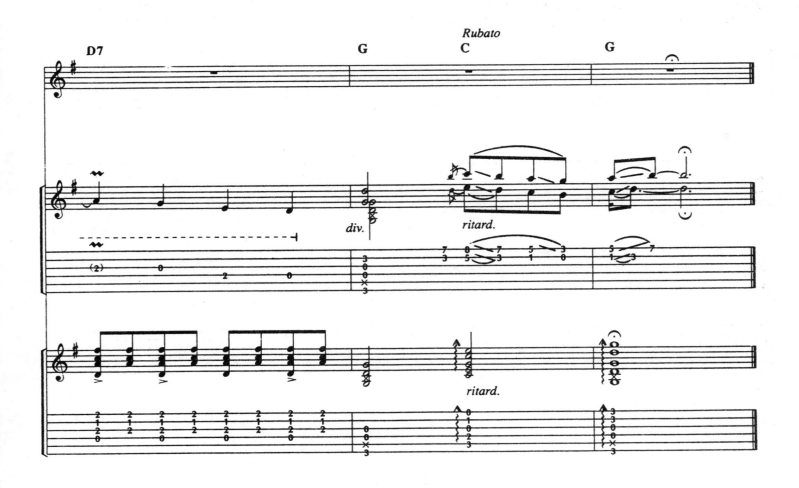

MY MAN

Words and Music by
BERNIE LEADON

*Pedal steel guitar arranged for Guitar 3 (⑥ = D ⑤ = G ④ = D ③ = G ② = B ① = D)

Verse 2:

once knew a man,___ a ver - y tal - ent - ed guy.___ He'd sing for the peo - ple and

peo - ple would cry.___ And know that his song___ came from deep, down in - side.___ You could

flow - er,____ he bloomed__ till that old,_____ hick - o - ry wind ____ called him home.____

Chorus:

My man's got it made.__ He's gone far be - yond__ the pain__

86

*Two guitars arranged for one.
**Another pedal steel Guitar arranged for Guitar 4 (⑥ = D ⑤ = G ④ = D ③ = G ② = B ① = D).

NEW KID IN TOWN

Words and Music by
JOHN DAVID SOUTHER
DON HENLEY and GLENN FREY

*Keyboard arranged for guitar.

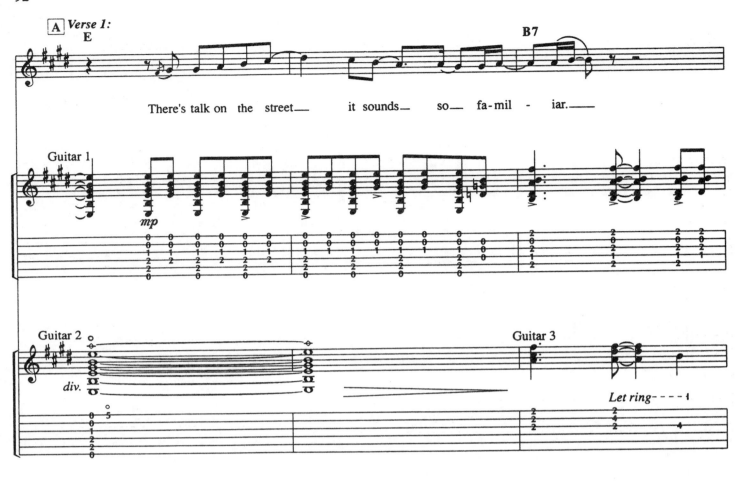

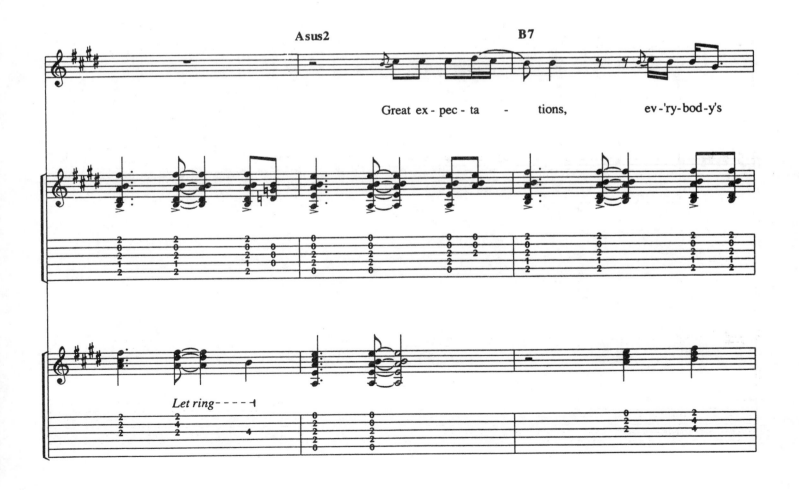

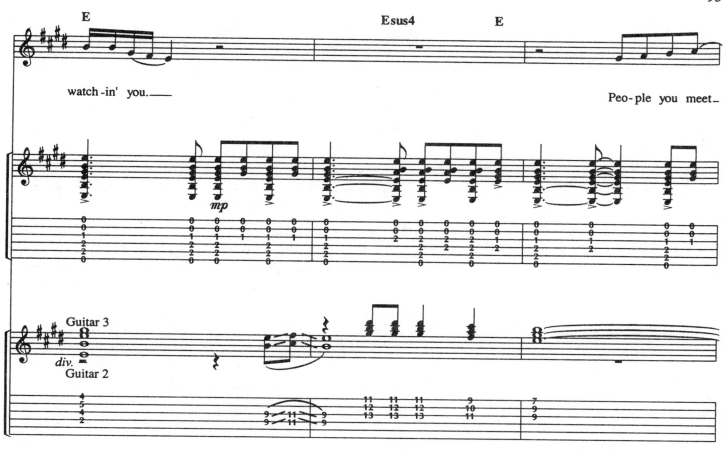

Verse 3:

There's talk on the street it's there to re-mind_____ you

Oo._____

that it does-n't real-ly mat - ter which side_____

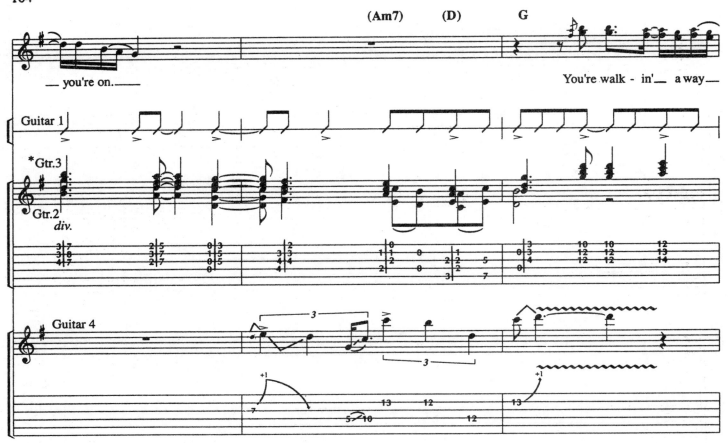

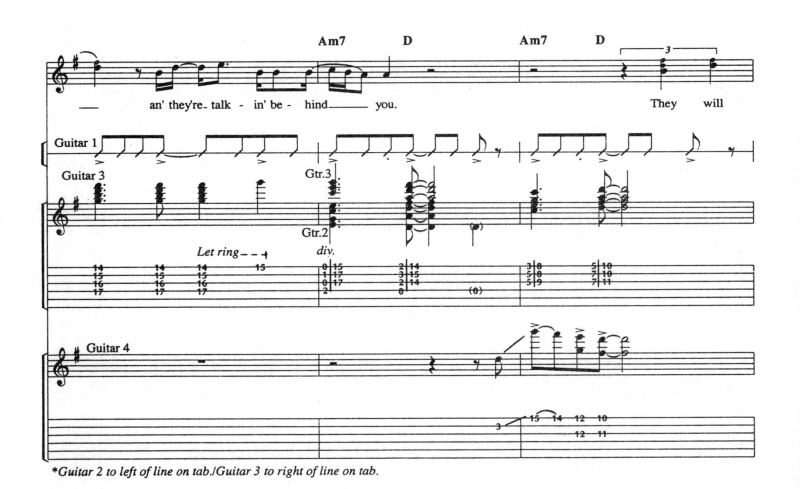

Guitar 2 to left of line on tab./Guitar 3 to right of line on tab.

never for-get you 'til some-bod-y new comes a-long.

Where you been late-ly? There's a new kid in

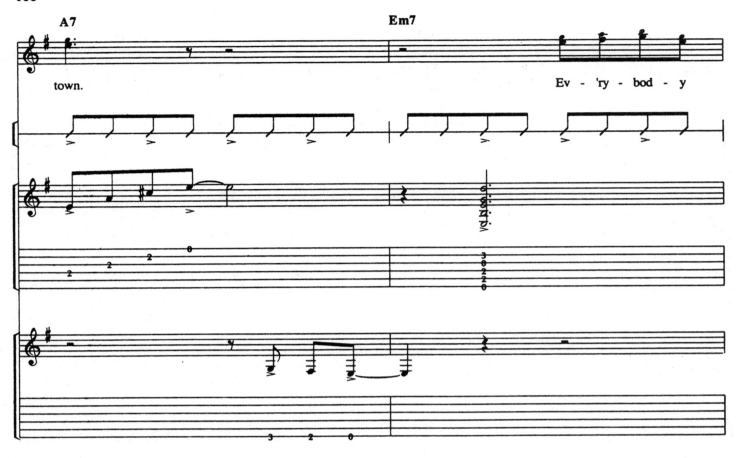

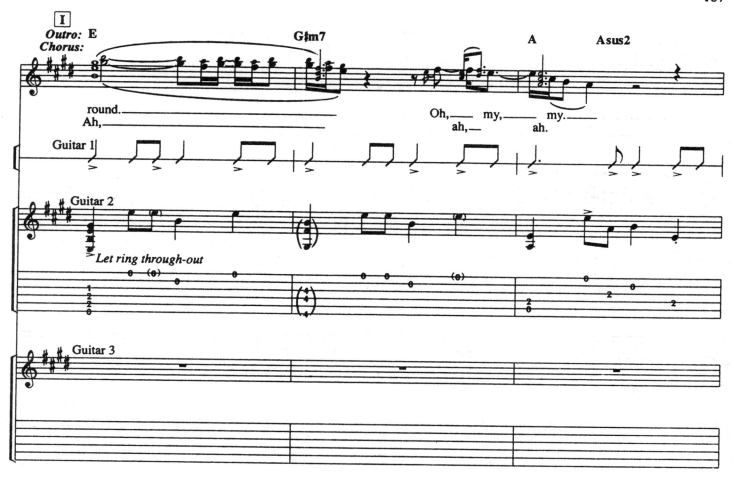

just an-oth-er new kid in town.

Ah.

ah.

ah,

ah.

ah.

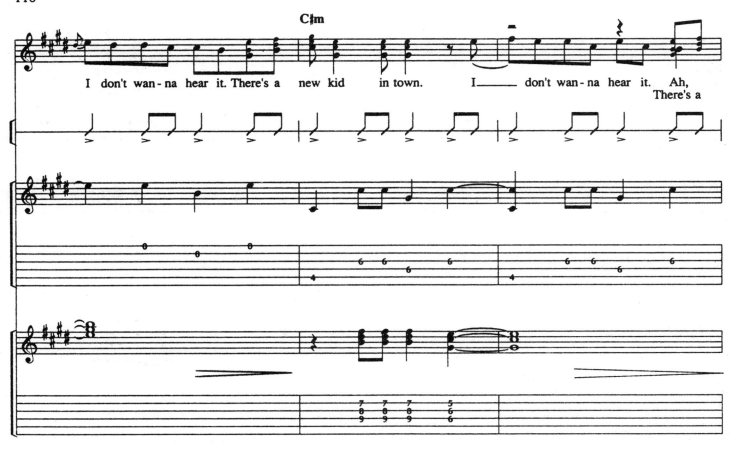

I don't wan-na hear it. There's a new kid in town. I____ don't wan-na hear it. Ah,
There's a

hoo!_____
new kid in town._____ There's a new kid in town.

There's a   new kid   in town.   Ev-'ry-bod-y's talk-in'.   There's a

new kid   in town.   Peo-ple start-ed walk-in'   There's a

112

OUTLAW MAN

Words and Music by
DAVID BLUE

114

Verse 1:
Rhythm Fig. 1

Guitar 1

I am an out-law, I was born an out-law's son.__ The high-way is my leg-a-cy__ on the

Guitar 2
Rhythm Fig. 1A

high-way I will run._____ In one hand I've a bi-ble,__ in the oth-er I've got a gun.__

End Rhythm Fig. 1   Chorus:

Ah don't you know__ me?__ I'm the man__ who won.____ Wo-man,__ don't try to love__ me, don't

End Rhythm Fig. 1A

try to un-der-stand.   A life__ up-on__ the road__ is the

116

Guitar Solo:
With Rhythm Figs. 1 & 1A

Chorus:

Wo - man,— don't try to love— me, don't try to un - der - stand.—

A life— up - on— the road— is the life of an out - law.—

TAKE IT EASY

Words and Music by
JACKSON BROWNE and GLENN FREY

Chorus:

don't e-ven try___ to un-der-stand.___ Just find a

place to make__ your__ stand___ and take it eas - y.___

end Rhy. Fig. 4

end Rhy. Fig. 4A

w/Riff A *(Gtr. 2)*
w/Rhy. Figs. 1 & 1A *(Gtrs. 1 & 3)*

Verse 2:
w/Rhy. Figs. 2 & 2A *simile (Gtrs. 1-3)*

(2.) Well, I'm a stand-in' on a cor-ner in Win-slow, Ar-i-zo-na___ an'

such a fine__ sight__ to see.___ It's a girl___ my__ Lord,___ in a flat__

124

Verse 3:

run-nin' down the road try'n'to loos-en my load,__ got a world__ of trou-ble on my__ mind. Look-
(Ooh,_____ ooh,   ooh,   ooh.

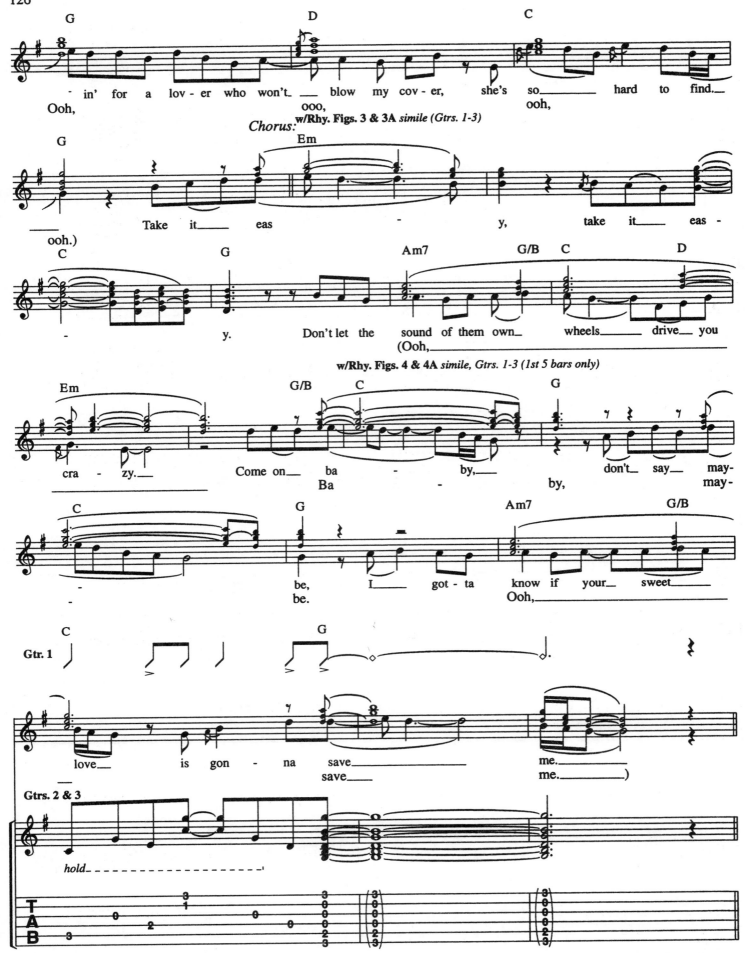

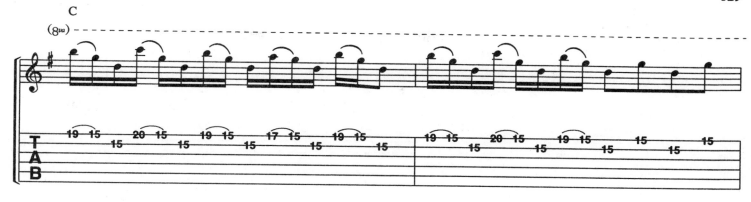

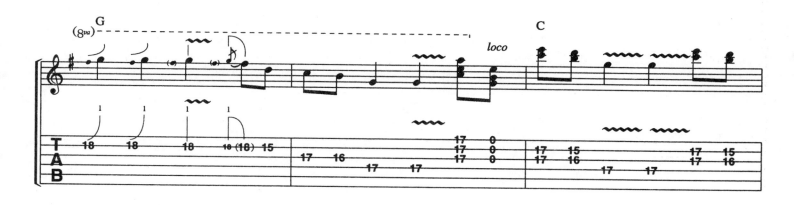

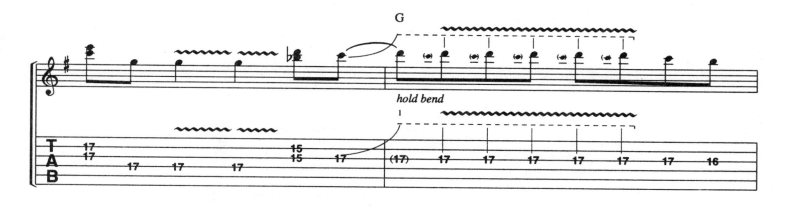

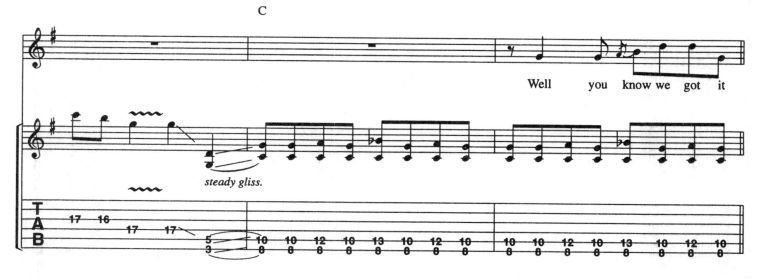

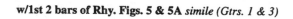

w/1st 2 bars of Rhy. Figs. 5 & 5A *simile (Gtrs. 1 & 3)*

Well you know we got it

steady gliss.

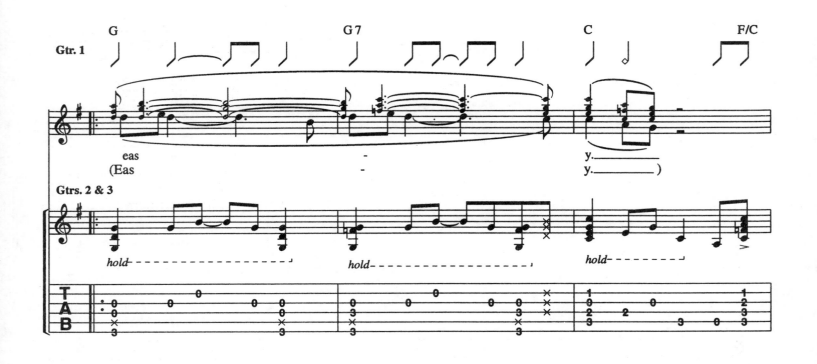

eas
(Eas -

y.
y.

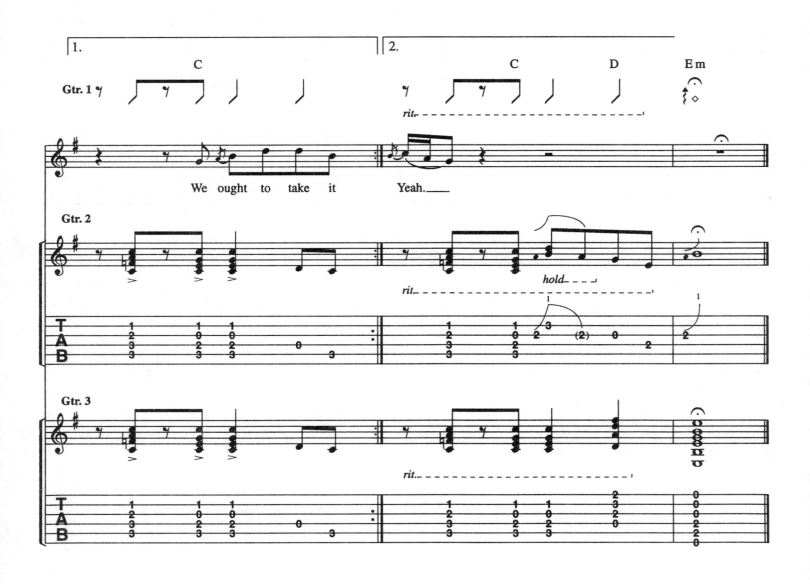

We ought to take it

Yeah.

TAKE THE DEVIL

Words and Music by
RANDY MEISNER

Moderately slow ♩ = 80

Intro:

O- pen up your eyes, take the dev - il from your mind._____

He's been hold - in' on____ to you,____ and you're____ so hard_____ to find._

Hit random open strings.

*Hit random open strings.

TEQUILA SUNRISE

**Words and Music by
DON HENLEY & GLENN FREY**

*Hammer to G6 chord w/index finger.

Verse 1:

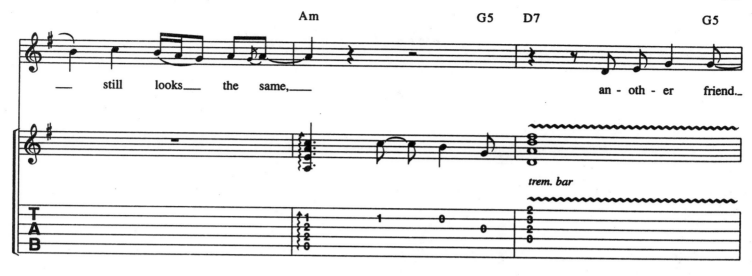

THE SAD CAFÉ

Words and Music by
DON HENLEY, GLENN FREY,
JOE WALSH and J.D. SOUTHER

149

And some of their dreams came true, and some just passed a-way.

And some of them stayed be-hind in-side the Sad Ca-fe.

The

TWENTY ONE

Words and Music by
BERNIE LEADON

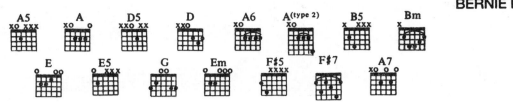

*Dobro arranged for Guitar 2 (G tuning: ⑥=D ⑤=G ④=D ③=G ②=B ①=D).

_____ my friends will be a - round. _____

should ev - er wan - na die.

GUITAR TAB GLOSSARY **

TABLATURE EXPLANATION

READING TABLATURE: Tablature illustrates the six strings of the guitar. Notes and chords are indicated by the placement of fret numbers on a given string(s).

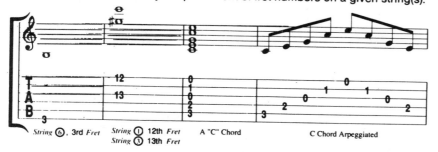

String ⑥, 3rd Fret *String ① 12th Fret* *String ③ 13th Fret* A "C" Chord   C Chord Arpeggiated

BENDING NOTES

HALF STEP: Play the note and bend string one half step.*

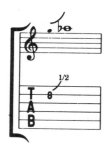

WHOLE STEP: Play the note and bend string one whole step.

WHOLE STEP AND A HALF: Play the note and bend string a whole step and a half.

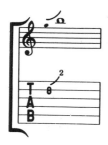

TWO STEPS: Play the note and bend string two whole steps.

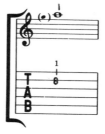

SLIGHT BEND (Microtone): Play the note and bend string slightly to the equivalent of half a fret.

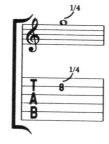

PREBEND (Ghost Bend): Bend to the specified note, before the string is picked.

PREBEND AND RELEASE: Bend the string, play it, then release to the original note.

REVERSE BEND: Play the already-bent string, then immediately drop it down to the fretted note.

BEND AND RELEASE: Play the note and gradually bend to the next pitch, then release to the original note. Only the first note is attacked.

BENDS INVOLVING MORE THAN ONE STRING: Play the note and bend string while playing an additional note (or notes) on another string(s). Upon release, relieve pressure from additional note(s), causing original note to sound alone.

BENDS INVOLVING STATIONARY NOTES: Play notes and bend lower pitch, then hold until release begins (indicated at the point where line becomes solid).

UNISON BEND: Play both notes and immediately bend the lower note to the same pitch as the higher note.

DOUBLE NOTE BEND: Play both notes and immediately bend both strings simultaneously.

*A half step is the smallest interval in Western music; it is equal to one fret. A whole step equals two frets.

© 1990 Beam Me Up Music
c/o CPP/Belwin, Inc. Miami, Florida 33014
International Copyright Secured   Made in U.S.A.   All Rights Reserved   **By Kenn Chipkin and Aaron Stang

RHYTHM SLASHES

STRUM INDICATIONS: Strum with indicated rhythm.

The chord voicings are found on the first page of the transcription underneath the song title.

INDICATING SINGLE NOTES USING RHYTHM SLASHES: Very often single notes are incorporated into a rhythm part. The note name is indicated above the rhythm slash with a fret number and a string indication.

ARTICULATIONS

HAMMER ON: Play lower note, then "hammer on" to higher note with another finger. Only the first note is attacked.

LEFT HAND HAMMER: Hammer on the first note played on each string with the left hand.

PULL OFF: Play higher note, then "pull off" to lower note with another finger. Only the first note is attacked.

FRET-BOARD TAPPING: "Tap" onto the note indicated by + with a finger of the pick hand, then pull off to the following note held by the fret hand.

TAP SLIDE: Same as fretboard tapping, but the tapped note is slid randomly up the fretboard, then pulled off to the following note.

BEND AND TAP TECHNIQUE: Play note and bend to specified interval. While holding bend, tap onto note indicated.

LEGATO SLIDE: Play note and slide to the following note. (Only first note is attacked).

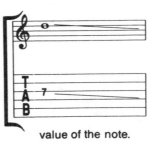

LONG GLISSANDO: Play note and slide in specified direction for the full value of the note.

SHORT GLISSANDO: Play note for its full value and slide in specified direction at the last possible moment.

PICK SLIDE: Slide the edge of the pick in specified direction across the length of the string(s).

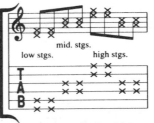

MUTED STRINGS: A percussive sound is made by laying the fret hand across all six strings while pick hand strikes specified area (low, mid, high strings).

PALM MUTE: The note or notes are muted by the palm of the pick hand by lightly touching the string(s) near the bridge.

TREMOLO PICKING: The note or notes are picked as fast as possible.

TRILL: Hammer on and pull off consecutively and as fast as possible between the original note and the grace note.

ACCENT: Notes or chords are to be played with added emphasis.

STACCATO (Detached Notes): Notes or chords are to be played roughly half their actual value and with separation.

DOWN STROKES AND UPSTROKES: Notes or chords are to be played with either a downstroke (⊓) or upstroke (∨) of the pick.

VIBRATO: The pitch of a note is varied by a rapid shaking of the fret hand finger, wrist, and forearm.

HARMONICS

NATURAL HARMONIC: A finger of the fret hand lightly touches the note or notes indicated in the tab and is played by the pick hand.

ARTIFICIAL HARMONIC: The first tab number is fretted, then the pick hand produces the harmonic by using a finger to lightly touch the same string at the second tab number (in parenthesis) and is then picked by another finger.

ARTIFICIAL "PINCH" HARMONIC: A note is fretted as indicated by the tab, then the pick hand produces the harmonic by squeezing the pick firmly while using the tip of the index finger in the pick attack. If parenthesis are found around the fretted note, it does not sound. No parenthesis means both the fretted note and A.H. are heard simultaneously.

TREMOLO BAR

SPECIFIED INTERVAL: The pitch of a note or chord is lowered to a specified interval and then may or may not return to the original pitch. The activity of the tremolo bar is graphically represented by peaks and valleys.

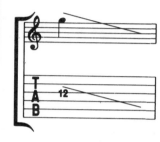

UN-SPECIFIED INTERVAL: The pitch of a note or a chord is lowered to an unspecified interval.